·KALEIDOSCOPE·

The Art of Illustrative Storytelling

GINGKO PRESS

KALEIDOSCOPE

The Art of Illustrative Storytelling

First Published in the USA by
Gingko Press by arrangement with
Sandu Publishing Co., Ltd.

Gingko Press, Inc.
1321 Fifth Street
Berkeley, CA 94710 USA
Tel: (510) 898 1195
Fax: (510) 898 1196
Email: books@gingkopress.com
www.gingkopress.com

ISBN 978-1-58423-689-4

Copyright © 2018 by Sandu Publishing
First published in 2018 by Sandu Publishing

Sponsored by Design 360°—
Concept and Design Magazine

Edited and produced by
Sandu Publishing Co., Ltd.

Book design, concepts & art direction by
Sandu Publishing Co., Ltd.
Chief Editor: Wang Shaoqiang
Design Director: Niu Huizhen

Illustration on front cover by Sehee Chae.
Illustration on back cover by Jasu Hu,
Sveta Dorosheva, Dung Ho, and Andrea De Santis.

info@sandupublishing.com
www.sandupublishing.com

Printed and bound in China

Contents

· 006   **Preface**

· 010   Whooli Chen

· 018   Kathrin Honesta

· 026   Alice Wellinger

· 034   Ruben Ireland

· 042   Lisk Feng

· 050   Eero Lampinen

· 058   Massimiliano di Lauro

· 064   Jasu Hu

· 070   Jesús Sotés Vicente

· 076   Miguel Montaner

· 082   Cinta Arribas

· 088   Stephan Schmitz

· 094   Chi Birmingham

· 098   Patrick Doyon

· 104   Teresa Bellon

· 110   Junkyard Sam

· 114   Federica Del Proposto

· 118   Sveta Dorosheva

· 124   Lieke van der Vorst

· 130   Marija Tiurina

· 134   Helena Perez Garcia   · 198   Jenn Liv

· 140   Sehee Chae   · 202   Dung Ho

· 146   Raúl Soria   · 208   Alice Yu Deng

· 152   Andrea De Santis   · 212   Paolo Domeniconi

· 158   Tristan Gion   · 218   Owen Gent

· 164   Tiago Galo   · 224   Linshu Zeng

· 170   Eleonora Arosio   · 230   Tina Siuda

· 176   Anna Pirolli

· 180   Shout

· 186   Taku Bannai   · 233   **Index**

· 192   Jeannie Phan   · 240   **Acknowledgements**

Preface

The Emphasis of Storytelling in Illustrations

Traditionally, illustrations are different because of their unique functionality. They used to play a vital role in books, newspapers, bibles, and children's books. Nowadays, narrative storytelling is a bit separated from editorial illustration education, because students get to choose between editorial illustration and illustrating for children's books. Producing a single image seems to be going in a conceptual direction, namely expounding on ideas, whereas illustrating children's books still requires traditional storytelling training. The concept of storytelling is easily understood, yet it is also one of the hardest things to put into a single art piece.

After I began grad school in the US, I began printmaking frequently and started to discover my unique interpretations of illustrations. When I finally graduated, I began to work with clients like *The New Yorker* and *The New York Times*. The content in the articles was sometimes fascinating to illustrate, but some sections were a bit dry. I tried very hard to make the illustrations fit the subject matter of the articles—and although the pictures that I produced for the clients were all acceptable quality for publication at that point, I found them to be very dull. To liven them up, I turned to brainstorming lists of ideas and found that my brain was full of stories. For example, I had a commission related to financial marketing, but I chose to draw something not directly connected to the article. Instead, I used my own stories and keywords to create an exciting scene of the ocean and a crowded boat—this showed the instability of the stock market. I just turned a wonky article into a metaphor and a piece of personal work, which also happened to work for the clients. Producing editorial illustrations is always a process of problem-solving, and brainstorming is only as difficult as the clients' ideas or the materials involved. That boat piece that I made was my breakthrough—it allowed me to change from being a drawing machine into a creator with my own style.

Storytelling is everywhere, not only in long-term projects. Conceptual illustrations can also be an excellent place to try out your narrative, because your audience is also imaginative.

Many art students and even some professional illustrators are on a long journey to seek out their personal styles. They like to ask question about it—for instance, "How does a successful illustrator make his/her work stand out among many others?" Your personal style is not an object to chase, nor it is a trendy thing you learn; it is you. What you experience and what you like influence your pieces; they trigger your motivation and inspiration, and your illustrations are utterly yours.

In this beautiful book, Shout's examples are peaceful and calm; his works are graphic, centralized, and balanced. When the audiences experienced his illustrations for diverse clients, they found them to be lonely, but they saw that the characters in the illustrations were enjoying the surroundings—as if the world that Shout created was for no one but themselves.

Massimiliano di Lauro's work, on the contrary, is bold, aggressive, and colorful. He likes to test different art materials. His pieces are each unique; every stroke is distinct. His work is not all about happiness—some pieces also have a tinge of anger or sadness—but the stories he tells all display strong character, which he cannot hide at all.

Eleanora Arosio's pieces seem incredibly naive—she even mentions this briefly in her section—her obsession with this word is central to her work. Naked ladies dance, float in space, and read on a sunny beach; her colored pencils document all these lighthearted moments. Becoming an adult is a dramatic change, and some people just forget about their inner naive self; Eleanora's works just remind viewers of this naiveté.

Can you imagine an illustrator creating work without having his/her own personal stories? I cannot. Storytelling lacks

methodology for illustrators, especially those who work for clients. We can find books about ways to illustrate children's books, fun ways to explore materials and sketches, or how to determine pricing and contract details when we are dealing with real jobs. But books that show us the process of producing a story methodology for single images are scarce, mainly because there is no one way to define a narrative for such pieces. Everyone has their own stories, and everyone's method of relating them in their illustrations is different, so there can be an uncountable number of concepts to discuss.

The aim of this book is not to show you any approach but to share the possibilities by introducing you to various artists who showcase their projects for distinct purposes. This book presents a splendid collection that readers can experience and use to communicate with the artists—they will get to know the artists' ways of depicting their styles, who they are, and what their stories are.

—Lisk Feng, The New York Studio
liskfeng.com

"
'How does a successful illustrator make his/her work stand out among many others?' Your personal style is not an object to chase, nor it is a trendy thing you learn; it is you.
"

Narrative and a bit surreal, I hope people can feel a poetic and whimsical moment in my work.

Whooli Chen

Whooli Chen is an illustrator based in Taiwan, and a member of the creative duo Sometime-Else Practice. She earned an MA degree in Illustration from the University of the Arts in London. During her stay in London, she spent the summer living near an urban fox. She missed the fox so much when she left that she began to draw under the name "Whooli," which translates to "fox" in Chinese.

Whooli found paintings enchanting from a very young age. "I guess that the reason why I chose fine arts is because I wanted to find out how those famous artworks were produced. How should I decide on a composition? How should I blend colors and match them with each other? How should I reproduce something I saw in life on a piece of paper?" said Whooli.

▲ Kishu An

Whooli Chen created the illustration "Kishu An" for Kishu An Forest of Literature's Anniversary Festival. Kishu An is a historic restaurant that stands not only as a historic building but as a landmark signifying Taiwan's post-war literature. The illustration is composed of Kishu An's typical riverside landscape, books, and festival events.

▲ 1. Fruit Is Love

"Fruit Is Love" is an illustration for a piece of prose about how the author discovered that offering a platter of fruits after dinner is a subtle gesture that expresses love in the family.

1. Where do you usually get inspiration?

Literature inspires me the most as it allows me to be amazed by every small detail in life. I am also addicted to collecting old Asian artwork, old Japanese woodblock printings, Persian miniatures, old Chinese Herbal Medicine drawings, ancient Buddhist paintings, and Western zoological prints.

2. You are part of the studio Sometime-Else Practice. What role does the studio play in your career?

Sometime-Else Practice is a side project that we established to break through our tedious day jobs. We just like the term "practice," and we hope that everything we do is a practice of expanding possibilities and an experiment of something new.

3. We notice that you have used an illustration from Blindness Series as your profile image. Does this series mean a lot to you? What is the story behind this series?

Blindness series is a self-initiated project. I often think that this series is the best representation of my daily life. I am not a very socially active person, so sometimes I am just like the portrait who somehow blocks herself from the outside, yet flourishes on her own.

4. Your drawings often contain a lot elements, like fruit, flowers, food, animals, etc. Do you have any principle on choosing these elements? Let's take Kishu An for example.

Usually there are certain elements that I need to use in order to represent the ideas of each illustration. But

I also consider elements that I am fond of personally. I like botanical elements, antique items, and old Asian paintings, so I had a lot of fun picking out an antique gourd-shaped vase from one of the paintings of the "Twelve Concubines of the Emperor Yongzheng," and placing it in Kishu An.

5. When illustrating for commercial and editorial projects, most illustrators are given a specific topic. How do you balance the client's demand and the freedom of creating?

I think it is crucial to build yourself a concise and refined portfolio, which will demonstrate your capability and style neatly. It can save you from running into lots of trouble when doing commissioned work. I prefer working on well-briefed projects—the client knows what they want, then I can develop more upon it.

6. Do you sometimes run into bottlenecks when illustrating? If so, what are they and how do you overcome them?

For me, the process of illustrating is a process of deliberation. I try very hard not to repeat the composition or the elements in my work. I believe that only through hard work can we overcome the anxiety of creation—for instance, by undergoing research as much as possible and executing the concept thoroughly and carefully. By doing this, I may have a chance to make a piece of work that I like.

▲ 2. Island of Dreams

"Kotoin" is a story about a lonely trip in Kyoto and the memory of visiting Kotoin, a sub-temple of Daitokuji.

"Blindness—Inner Garden Series" is a project consisting of three portraits, which portray the concept of lonely modern life—we are often absorbed in our blind yet complacent inner world and try to flourish a private garden.

◄ 1. Kotoin
▼ 2. Blindness: Psychic Friends

◂ 3. Blindness: Isolated Playground
▾ 4. Blindness: Distant Iceberg
▾ 5. Blindness: Isolated Playground (Details)
▾ 6. Blindness: Distant Iceberg (Details)

"Sojourner" is an illustration describing an author's memory of recuperating from illness and being forced to stay at home. It is about the experience of sojourning in a place we are so familiar with but we rediscover everything around us in a new and strange way.

"Clustered Sweetness of Life" is a story about taking a trip to Tokyo in autumn and finding out that life is just on a dinner tray.

▲ 1. Felicity's House
▶ 2. Sojourner

Dreamy, whimsical, delicate with a hint of faith, depth, darkness, and a sense of longing.

Kathrin Honesta

Kathrin Honesta is an Indonesian-born graphic designer and illustrator. Growing up in a family that had little connection to art, Kathrin became interested in picture books and comics at a very young age. She drew her own comic series and knew with conviction that art was something that she wanted to pursue in the future. She has since spent five years studying and working in Malaysia. The people in that country inspired her and reminded her to always be more open-minded and view things from different perspectives. Her illustrations are stories about faith and people. She realizes that a piece of artwork is not about just being pretty aesthetically but is about the message that it is conveying. Currently she is settling in Jakarta, Indonesia.

Pencils and pens are Kathrin's favorite tools, as she enjoys the raw textures that these tools present. When she is not using those, she draws digitally using Photoshop most of the time, and the process is much quicker. It is always an exciting thing for Kathrin to mix different techniques and do some experiments.

▲ Drowning in Thoughts

1. Tell us a little about your illustrating process.

The process varies depending on the kind of project that I am going to work on. It starts mostly with an ideation or brainstorming stage, where I tend to get away from the screen and scribble mainly on paper. By working this way, I feel that ideas come up easier. After I get the rough sketches, I gain the inspiration I need from books, music, stories from friends, architecture, fabric patterns, nature, or online. Then I start to execute the final illustration.

2. A female character is an often-seen topic in your work. Could you share with us the concept behind it?

Drawing is the way I express myself, including my thoughts, questions, and dreams. It is like a sort of self-reflection. This is probably why in most of my personal drawings there are faces of women. I think that is how I reflect myself. I want to draw something that I am related to and that I resemble.

3. When illustrating, do you sometimes run into bottlenecks? If so, what are they and how do you overcome them?

Of course I do! Once in a while I experience a stage in which drawing is not fun at all. But I view it as a normal stage that I must overcome. Therefore, the first thing I have to remind myself is not to panic but instead to handle it calmly. Usually when such negative emotions occur, I stop working for a while, and go out and get myself buried in other things, like hanging out with friends, reading books, doing grocery shopping, driving around, watching a movie, etc. When I feel better after that, I can start working again.

▼ 1. Between Me and You

growing

▲ 2. Growing in Him

4. Are there any particular illustrators or designers who have influenced you?

I can think of so many, but to name just a few, Isabelle Arsenault, Edward Gorey, Lisk Feng, and Maurice Sendak are my favorites!

5. What are your words of wisdom?

"Love the Lord your God with all your heart and with all your soul and with all your strength and with all your mind" and "Love your neighbor as yourself." Those verses are from the Bible and I keep them in my heart and strive to apply them to my life.

"Out Growing" expresses the feeling of being out of one's comfort zone.

▲ 1. Outgrowing
▶ 2. The Undaunted Dandelion: Relaxing

▲ 3. The Moon Girl

"Path" shows Kathrin's faith: Light will guide you home.

"The Undaunted Dandelion" is an on-going project about a character called the undaunted dandelion and her journey.

▲ 2. The Undaunted Dandelion: Discovery
◀ 3. The Undaunted Dandelion: Pet Turtle

Thought-provoking. My artwork addresses controversial topics and problems of our society in a surreal way.

Alice Wellinger

As a self-taught illustrator, Alice Wellinger calls herself a late starter. She has worked as a graphic designer for many years. After she gave birth to her twin girls, she began to write and illustrate children's books. Although these books got published and won some awards, Alice kept eye for new shores. A few years ago, she started to work as an editorial illustrator. "I like doing this because of the artistic freedom it offers me (most of the time at least). Each commission is a new challenge for me," said Alice. She believes that the most important thing about an illustration is the concept; all the visual elements have to support the idea itself.

▲ Sleepless Nights

"Sleepless Nights" and "Sinking Boat" are a
series of illustrations for an article, "The Burden
of Debts," published on *Migros Magazine*.

▲ 1. Sinking Boat

1. You worked as a graphic designer before becoming an illustrator. How come you made this choice?

In the 1980s when I was pursuing my study, illustration was not very popular in Austria. I never thought of making a living as an illustrator. I was told that as a graphic designer, I would be drawing and painting a lot, which was, of course, wrong. Nevertheless, I enjoyed that profession for more than 15 years before I finally made up my mind to be an illustrator.

2. What materials and tools do you enjoy working with the most? Why?

Acrylics, pencils, color pencils, and ink. I like using the tools that allow me to draw fast; also I like showing variety in my work by using different tools and techniques.

3. Where do you usually get inspiration?

I usually find inspiration while working.

4. Tell us a little about your illustrating process. What is your favorite part?

Sometimes I have a certain picture in my mind, which will be a direct path from scribble to finished artwork. But most of the time, I have to search for ideas just like every artist does by brainstorming, scribbling, reflecting, and thinking. I like the moment when a good idea comes up like a tiny shining star in the night sky.

5. Do you sometimes run into bottlenecks when illustrating? If so, what are they and how do you overcome them?

It took me quite a while to understand that doubt,

failure, and corrections are normal side effects of the creative process. All I should do is to accept it and keep going.

6. Are there any particular illustrators or designers who have inspired you?

I would like to take the opportunity to draw attention to a few extraordinary female illustrators: Rotraut Susanne Berner and Susanne Janssen, both famous for their unique children's book illustrations; Bianca Tschaikner, illustrator and world-traveler; Lika Nüsslia, Swiss illustrator and crossover-artist; Stephanie Wunderlich, Maira Kalman, Sabine Timm, and so on. You can also find many more great artists on the Tumblr blog named "Dark Silence in Suburbia."

7. Do you have any words of wisdom for those who are on their way to becoming illustrators?

I would share Astrid Lindgren's words: "Don't let them get you down. Be cheeky, wild, and wonderful!"

▶ 2. Abortion

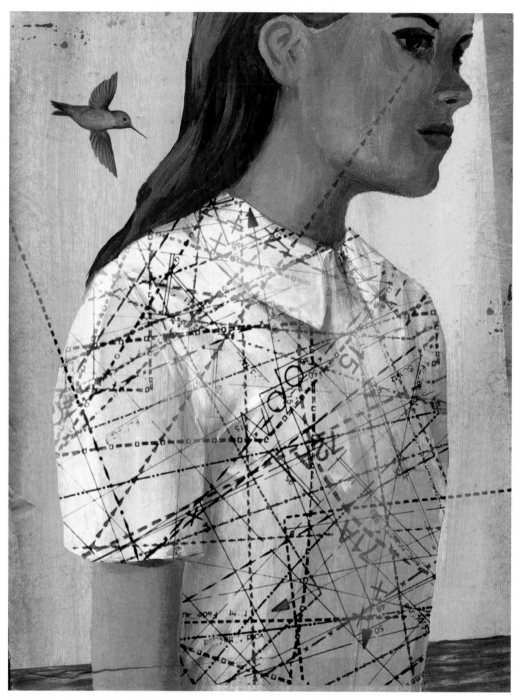

▲ 1. Life Plan

"Lies and Spines" and "A Part of Me" are part of a book of illustrations for the Othello Series. This series is part of a project named "SHAKESPEARE," launched by some artists including Alice Wellinger. The aim of this project is to interpret females' roles in Shakespeare's works in a novel, narrative, and artistic way.

▲ 2. Lies and Spines
▲ 3. A Part of Me
▼ 4.& 5. A Part of Me (Details)

 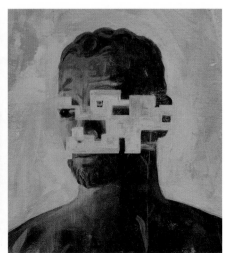

▲ 1. Horse Girl

▲ 2. Magician

◄ 3. Magician (Detials)

"Horse Girl" and "Magician" are illustrations of characters for "Freudenhaus Circus Festival."

"Drinking Mother" is an editorial illustration for an article published by *Migros Magazine* about how it is impossible to be a good mother as an alcohol addict.

▲ 4. Drinking Mother

I see my work as minimalist stylized portraiture that uses emotional and cultural symbolism to explore our inner and outer worlds and the relationships between the two.

Ruben Ireland

Ruben Ireland is an illustrator and artist based in the UK. He was raised by creative parents who encouraged him to pursue all his interests as a child. As a teenager he was interested in acting and fine art as well as cinema, but he finally decided to study Illustration at university because he ended up enjoying storytelling more than the rest.

Ruben creates dreamlike portraits by using mixed media, both traditional and digital, like Photoshop and Corel Painter, to depict the tale of the inner self—fragility, strength, and solitude.

Although his work process is more involved in digital aspects for the sake of getting the final look he wants, he has always loved ink the most. For him, ink has a beautiful fluidity, while giving such a perfect denseness in its finish. He uses acrylic paints as well—they are what he grew up using. "Although they bear a range of limitations compared to oil paints, I am much more comfortable with acrylic, particularly during the sketching stages," Ruben mentioned.

This is an illustration created for Playing Arts, a playing card set designed by 55 selected international artists.

▲ Four of Hearts

▲ 1. Fortune

1. You were born and grew up in Amsterdam. Why did you choose to settle in the UK? What aspects of the life and culture there influence you and your work?

I lived in the Netherlands until I was seven, when my family packed up and moved to England for a holiday, which in the end turned into a permanent move. Although I still feel a strong connection to my very early childhood, I would say that my experiences in the British countryside and then eventually my adulthood in London have influenced my work most, particularly the solitude and natural beauty of the countryside, married with the style and social dynamics of London.

2. Tell us a little about your illustrating process.

How I put down ideas varies depending on what I want to create or who the client might be. I always like to begin with pencil, ink, and acrylic to create a general composition and palette. Then I rough out a more detailed portrait and start to clean up sketches, which can be scanned into the computer. When the sketches are scanned, I use Photoshop and Corel Paint to further compose and clean up the image before working on more details on a number of layers. It can take me weeks to a month for each image, depending on the complexity and size. In the end, I create some hand-made textural

sheets with ash, papers, water, spray paints, or whatever I have around me. I then scan and apply them to some sections of the nearly finished image.

3. Female portraits and animals in black and white tones seem to be signature motifs in your work, so what do you want to convey most through your art?

Feminine beauty has always captured me in its ability to express so much meaning and emotion with such elegance and strength. My use of animals is often symbolic, allowing me to express cultural and metaphysical contemplation. In terms of aesthetics, using stark contrasting tones and silhouette forms exaggerates the things that lie between, which ends up being the subtle grays that hold dominance of a space mostly made up of blacks and whites.

4. We noticed that your work "Marianna" has received many likes online, like Society6, Instagram, and so on. Could you tell us something more about this illustration?

It is amazing to see just how well "Marianna" has been received. It was a collaboration between artist Jenny Liz Rome and I a few years ago. We had no plan about what we wanted to create but just enjoyed merging both of our styles. I started drawing the girl and Jenny created the headpiece for her. To me, I always imagine a woman standing on a cliff edge, waiting for her long lost lover to return from the sea.

5. *What do you consider to be your proudest achievement so far as an artist?*

I try to celebrate all the good things that have happened. My show in San Francisco was a real high point. Gauntlet Gallery over there let me invite a group of my favorite artists to show their work, so I ended up going back to San Francisco for a few months because I loved the city and the gallery so much. I also had a really great time traveling to Paris and Munich to work with Juniqe and Jaguar, and I met some great illustrators and photographers there. Anything that involves traveling really makes me happy.

6. *Are there any illustrators or designers who you admire and look up to?*

I am a huge fan of Dieter Braun, who I had the chance to spend time with in Paris and Munich. I am also very fond of Ernst Haeckel, Riikka Sormunen, Ermsy, Olaf Hajek, Alessandra Maria, Fuco Ueda, and so many that I could go on forever!

7. *What else are you keen on?*

Cycling has become my other passion. There is nothing better than putting headphones on and taking long bike rides through London. Besides that, I am really enjoying renovating a boat, which has taught me about woodwork, electricity, and plumbing. Creating my own functional and beautiful space from scratch is incredibly satisfying, and life on the water is really liberating.

▼ 2. The Mound

▲ 1. Skyling

"Skyline" is about a performer resting in quiet moments away from the crowd.

"Quiet Echoes" shows a place for solitude one finds in quiet echoes and silent wilds.

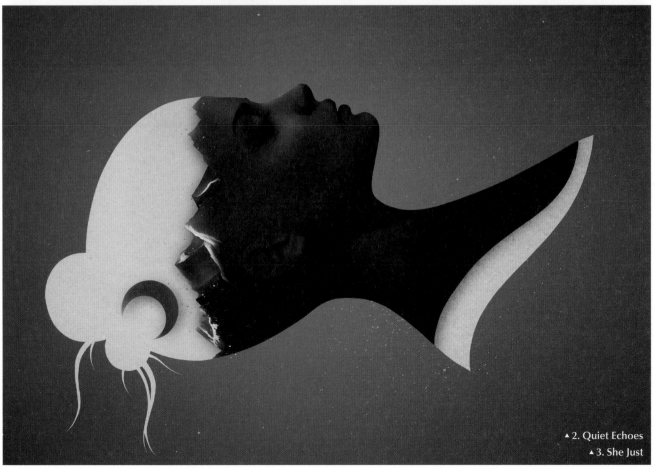

▲ 2. Quiet Echoes
▲ 3. She Just

"News from Afar" is about the feeling of being called from afar by a lost lover. Each quiet whisper brings comfort and fleeting hope.

Ruben created "Marianna" in collaboration with the artist Jenny Liz Rome.

▲ 1. Chorum
▶ 2. News from Afar

▲ 3. Marianna

I normally create works with limited color palettes. Because I am a huge fan of screen printing, I like adding a touch of screen printing in my work, which I hope is narrative, whimsical, and conceptual.

Lisk Feng

Originally from China, Lisk Feng is an award-winning illustrator based in New York. She graduated with an MFA in Illustration Practice from the Maryland Institute College of Art in 2014. She illustrates mostly for newspapers, magazines, and publications such as *The New York Times, The New Yorker, The Washington Post, The Wall Street Journal, Wired, Penguin*, and so on.

Lisk's parents are both artists. Her mother works as an art teacher; her father was in an underground rock band and is now a digital media artist doing experimental performances.

Thus when Lisk decided to be an illustrator, her parents never said "no" to her choice, but instead they supported her on every level.

Growing up in a small, beautiful, yet isolated town, Lisk's memory of drawing dates back to her grandparents' backyard packed with flowers and animals. Her grandpa used blackboard paint to cover the wooden door that was used to separate the animals and plants. The painted door then became Lisk's canvas. During summer time, she would sit under the sun with plants and animals, doodling on the blackboard, drawing a fake island or designing her own kingdom.

▲ Goddess's New Clothes

"Goddess's New Clothes" is an illustration about
a sunny afternoon where you are wearing your
favorite clothes and enjoying your own little time.

▲ 1. Oh, Perfect Life 1

1. Where do you usually get inspiration?

The Internet is a decent place for me to get the information I need immediately. It is an extremely handy tool nowadays. I am also a book lover who enjoys reading old novels like *1984* and *The Shinning*, and of course children's novels are required reading for creating narrative illustrations. Recently I reread E. Nesbit's books, which kind of allowed me to relive my childhood. Kids, adventure, and the feel of summer are what drive me to illustrate.

2. Currently you live and work in the US, does life there influence you and your creation?

New York City is wonderful. I wish I could draw all of its diversity into my illustrations. I am a huge fan of music and movies, and New York provides the best place to experience hard to find concerts and moving pictures. The energetic style of living as much art as I can gives me energy to create in this city.

3. You have worked with many publishers and clients. Which one most impressed you? Why? Is there any publisher or client with whom you want to collaborate in the future?

I really love working with Matt Dorfman. He is an art director for *The New York Times*'s book review. He gives artists total freedom but still keeps them close to the main point. Illustrators can also make suggestions about and be involved in the page design so that the texts and images can be connected, rather than isolated from each other.

I wish I could do a cover illustration for AD Paul Buckley from Penguin once. His covers are amazing.

4. Do you have a method for choosing elements like color palette, characters, and composition for your illustrations?

I love using a creamy off-white for the background. And I love creating vintage compositions while adding some new flavors to each piece. Geometric shapes help making my work simple and stronger. That is basically what I am attempting in all my illustrations.

5. Do you have any plans or wishes for your future work or life? Please share some with us.

I am currently illustrating my first children's book called *Everest*. I never thought I could handle long-term projects because of my impatient personality; therefore in the past, I have always done editorial illustration. But at the end of last year I felt burned out after tons of short-turn-around projects, and my work showed my exhaustion. So I took the book job and spent several months straight researching and brainstorming. It is still in progress, but I am super excited about it. Once I slow down, my thinking becomes better. I have recently realized that my brain needs a different kind of working mode once in a while so I can get back on track and produce strong work.

6. Do you have any words of wisdom for those who are on their ways to becoming illustrators?

Believe in your work. Love what you do.

"Oh, Perfect Life" is a series of illustrations with a seasonal theme for *Readers Campus* covers. Each cover depicts an illustration that gives a feel for the given month.

◄ 2. Oh, Perfect Life 2

"Hello Kongzi" is an illustration series for a project called Hello Kongzi. It showcases the five traditional virtues proposed by Confucius: Benevolence, Justice, Courtesy, Wisdom, Sincerity. The whole series was projected on the wall of Grand Central Station, New York.

▲ 1. Oh, Perfect Life 3
◄ 2. Oh, Perfect Life 4

▲ 3. Hello Kongzi: Justice

1. Hello Kongzi: Sincerity
2. Hello Kongzi: Courtesy
3. Hello Kongzi: Wisdom

I like to have a certain tension in my drawings, like something bad is about to happen. It creates a narrative into the illustration that expands beyond the image itself. Sadness is a captivating riddle that arouses our curiosity.

Eero Lampinen

Eero Lampinen has always drawn and painted obsessively. He grew up in Belgium, learned how to draw comics, and later studied graphic design in Helsinki, Finland. He is now an illustrator based in that city. "I think that illustration just fits the way I like to express myself, so it has been a very natural vocation that I have rarely had to question. If I was not an illustrator, I would like to be a dancer or a florist," said Eero.

He usually works with ink, brushes, watercolor, and an eerie digital color palette. His work is an intriguing blend of folklore and pop culture, often depicting offbeat characters in adjacent realities. Sugar coated hues and modern decorative details of his work accentuate the tone for his dreamlike scenarios that blur the lines between fantasy and reality.

▲ Mermaids

▲ 1. Depletion

1. We know that Scandinavian design is characterized by simplicity and minimalism. Does this trend have any influence on you and your work?

I love the work of other Finnish illustrators and my peers inspire me a lot, but I hope that my work does not fit into the Scandinavian design narrative. While I want my work to have simple concepts and color palettes, I also want to embrace maximalism, cheesy sincerity, perhaps even kitsch. I am not the kind of person who likes curating or collecting things. I love plants but I do not like designer homes. I own very little, and I buy objects and clothes out of necessity rather than for their design. What I like about our time is that you can create things virtually. What excites me about art is creating imaginary worlds, instead of material things.

2. What materials and tools do you enjoy working with the most? Why?

I am some sort of a perfectionist, so I love using the eraser and drawing things many times over. For a long time I really loved working with ink and brush, but at the moment I am taking a break from that and using pencils

for my digital work. I am pushing myself to try new techniques and not limit myself only to certain tools, but at the same time keep the process fun and interesting.

3. Tell us a little about your illustrating process.

I make a lot of very loose sketches and doodles, especially faces based on photographs or people I meet. A drawing usually starts from a face that I like and a vague image in my head. After a few thumbnail sketches, I start building the composition, adding and removing things as I go along. I always work with a light box and paper in A2 size. When the sketch is done, I either ink or draw the clean line art on a separate paper using the light box, then I scan the line art and add color and textures with Photoshop.

4. You said that mythology and folktales inspire you. Can you tell us more about this?

I like the way folktales were used to explain everyday life through fantastic allegories. I think that I am particularly interested in magic realism, little supernatural details in a realistic context. Even though I am quite a realist personally, I tend to interpret life through the lens of superstition and magic. I think it is possible to be both superstitious and realistic at the same time—a lot of the things that we know are contradictory, and some are beyond our capacity to understand—so why not embrace it?

5. What kind of person do you think you are? How is your personality reflected in your work?

I have a tendency to be inside my own head a lot, and this is sometimes reflected in the characters that I draw. I like stories of outcasts and marginal characters, or of sensitive anti-heroes, or people who do not fit into any particular mold. So in my drawings, I explore sensitivity and softness. I am a bit chaotic and disorganized, so maybe for that reason I like my work to be very clean with sharp details and clean line art, just for balance.

6. When illustrating, do you sometimes run into bottlenecks? If so, what are they and how do you overcome them?

Yes, from time to time! Commissioned work where the client asks you to work outside your comfort zone can be a great opportunity for learning and challenging yourself, but it can also be very draining at the same

time. Often it is hard to take some time off, especially as a freelancer. But it is absolutely necessary to distance yourself from your work from time to time to get new energy and ideas. When struggling with an idea, I try to allow myself to draw something completely unrelated, or I leave the studio altogether even though it is counter-intuitive and difficult to do when you have a deadline approaching. I recently returned from a three-month-residency in Taiwan and have since found my work evolving in new directions.

7. Are there any illustrators or designers who you admire or look up to?

Growing up, I think Winsor McCay's *Little Nemo in Slumberland* had a strong influence on me, as well as Taiyo Matsumoto's comics, Jamie Hewlett's *Tank Girl,* and Sophie Campbell's comic *Wet Moon*. Out of more current artists I love the work of David Rappeneau and Yoko Kuno.

8. What else are you keen on aside from design and illustration?

I love dancing, and I wish that I had time to take more dance classes. Other than that, I love cooking and spending time around animals.

▶ 2. Feeding Hour

▲ 1. Insect Collector

"Rakkautta & Anarkiaa" is a promotional illustration
for the 29th Helsinki International Film Festival.

▲ 1. No More Tears

▶ 2. Leisure Pursuit

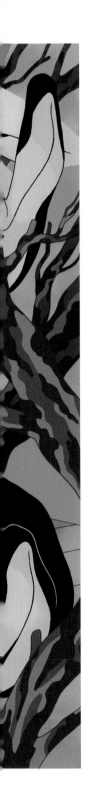

"No More Tears" and "Leisure Pursuit" are personal
works by Eero. He tries to create marginal characters
to explore sensitivity and softness.

I test a lot of stuff and continually try to get out of my comfort zone. Strong and aggressive creatures, irony, and brilliant colors are the constant elements in my works.

Massimiliano di Lauro

Born in Trani, Italy in 1984, Massimiliano di Lauro has been enamored with drawing since he was a child. Marker pens were his favorite toys while he was growing up. One day he stepped into a beautiful bookstore and purchased a picture book. He was totally captivated by the illustrations in this book and thought to himself that he wanted to be an illustrator. But life is never a straight path to one's destination. Though he graduated from the Polytechnic University of Bari with a diploma in Industrial Design, he felt that he had failed in his dream of being an illustrator. So he started to search and study, bought numerous books, went to fairs, and kept drawing. He now draws with every kind of tool—markers, ink, crayons— and uses many mediums including watercolor, monotype, and digital media.

He gets inspiration from everywhere—people in the bar, movies and arts that he loves, and even the work of other illustrators—everything that he has captured with his eyes and every story that he has heard on the streets can be an element in his work. Massimiliano believes in what Pablo Picasso said: "Good artists copy, great artists steal," which to him means great artists will absorb and learn from others and then transform the things they have learned into something new, something of their own, through their creative process.

In February 2012, Massimiliano published his first picture book titled *Mi Primer Viaje* in collaboration with OQO Editora, which was translated in Spanish, Galician, Italian, French, and Portuguese. His works have been published by magazines like *Scientific American*, *Corriere della Sera*, and *Rock Motel*, as well as by children's book publishers in Europe and Asia.

"Lucca Junior" tells a story about a child living in his small room dreaming about exploring the strange wilds and far-away islands.

▲ Lucca Junior

"Valentine's Day" is an illustration for an article about the romantic gifts and dress codes for Valentine's Day published by *Corriere della Sera*. The sweetness of love is well depicted through the affectionate pink color. Loving couples of diverse ages and sexes show their love in unique ways.

▲ Valentine's Day

As a music enthusiast himself, Massimiliano created "Josh Homme" as a tribute to the history of rock music. Josh Homme is a member of the band Queens of the Stone Age.

"Original Italian: Sanguinaccio" was created for an exhibition about food and humans' relationship with it. Sanguinaccio is a traditional Italian recipe made with chocolate and pig blood—a carnival dessert.
To extract blood from a pig, generally the pig has to be slaughtered slowly. Massimiliano captures this cruel scene through an amusing picture, in order to illustrate a bitter fact: we are what we eat.

▲ 2. Passive Aggressive

▶ 3. Original Italian: Sanguinaccio

I regard myself as an emotional thinker, a lover of simplicity and strong conceptual ideas. My work is evolving as much as I am growing myself.

Jasu Hu

Jasu Hu is a Chinese-born illustrator based in New York. She studied Visual Communication Design and Illustration at Tsinghua University and at the Maryland Institute College of Art. Since she graduated she has been working as a freelance illustrator, taking her particular perspective into elegant, emotional, and conceptual illustrations. Dedicated to print and digital media, Jasu believes illustration is the strongest way to solve visual problems.

Growing up, Jasu was a shy girl. Drawing was the only way that she could express her feelings and thoughts and communicate with others. She was obsessed with Japanese manga when she was young, dreamt about being a professional comic artist, and kept practicing her drawing skills. She barely knew anything about illustration until she went to the university. When she drew, one of her classmates asked: "Are you making an illustration?" It was not until then that she realized how much she was into drawing images.

Graphic design and its philosophy influence Jasu as an illustrator. Just like the recognized American designer Paul Rand once said: "Design is so simple, that's why it's so complicated." Jasu's work stands out with its simple composition and flat colors, yet sophisticated theme.

Reading is another main source of inspiration for Jasu; it feeds her imagination. For her, fictional narratives stimulate her imagination while nonfiction introduces concepts to her that help her practice brainstorming.

Jasu enjoys working digitally with her Wacom tablet and pens, which are clean, convenient, fast, and easy to make adjustments to. She likes making her own textures and brush stokes with traditional tools as well.

"Recordkeeping Fees" is an illustration for an article about a variety of payment structures available to financial plans published by *PLANSPONSOR*.

▲ Recordkeeping Fees

▲ 1. The Sound of Silence

"The Sound of Silence" is a cover illustration for a book review about Elizabeth Strout's novel *My Name Is Lucy Barton*, a personal story about urban loneliness and deep emotion.

"The Magician" is for an article about Adam Grant, a workplace magician, who wrote books to reveal his secrets of originality to the public, published by *The New York Times*.

"Wall Street Bro Talk" is for an article about sexism and bro talk on Wall Street, published by *The New York Times*.

▲ 2. The Magician
▼ 3. Wall Street Bro Talk

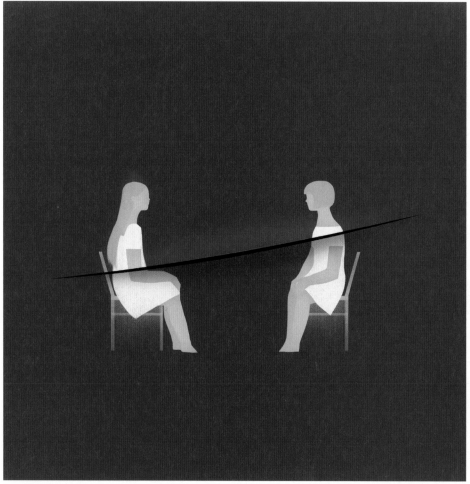

"The Book She Left Behind" is for an essay written by the novelist Tom Rachman. Tom wrote about his sister, who died young of cancer, and how he learned about his sister after her passing through her extensive book collections.

▲ 3. A Job That Nourishes the Soul
◄ 4. The Book She Left Behind

Bold and very colorful; a little dark and a little sad. There is almost a touch of humor in my work.

Jesús Sotés Vicente

Jesús Sotés Vicente has always drawn everywhere and all the time. He grew up as a typical child, one who ended up doodling on everything that fell into his hands, which made it a natural choice for him to become an illustrator. Without a doubt, brushes are the tool that he enjoys to work with most. He feels that hand-drawn art is the natural way for him to reconnect with the essence of drawing, which is always a real pleasure for him. "Working with brushes makes me feel like coming back home," said Jesús. He tries to get inspiration from all those famous artists who have opened doors and taken new roads ahead of him because he believes that great masters are always the best source of inspiration. He says: "We only need to look back and learn." Aside from the great minds, many other things inspire him including films, music, reading, nature, people, and travels.

DAY OF THE BOOK

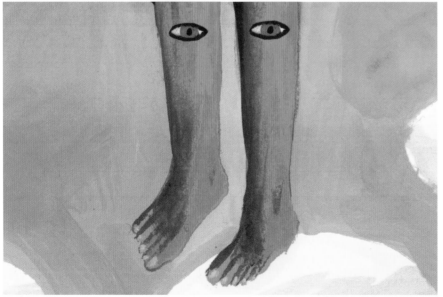

All these illustrations are part of Jesús's daily work. They are taken from his workbooks or sketchbooks. Bold brushes and strong colors are allied to tell a story and depict the characters.

▲ 3. This Is Not My Soap 01
▶ 4. This Is Not My Soap 02

▲ 1. Let the Bugs Fly

▲ 2. Trumpet Solo

◄ 3. Vulkania (The Fire Inside Us)

▴ 4. Lonely Figure Dressed in Red with Swallows

My work is like a shorter path to understanding an idea. My illustrations are actually visual paths that I create to lead viewers to get to the idea. All the graphics are centered on this concept—bold, minimal, and direct.

Miguel Montaner

Miguel Montaner was born and grew up by the sea, only a stone's throw away from Barcelona. He began drawing as a child in his free time with his elder sister. As he grew up, he started experimenting with the communicative function of images through trial and error. Since very few academic courses in illustration are offered in Spain, Miguel is not formally trained but rather self-taught. "I became an illustrator thanks to a mix of effort and randomness," he claims.

Miguel is constantly trying to find the balance between reflection and execution, concept and aesthetics in his work. He usually uses paper and pen to draw quick notes about ideas and then works with digital tools like a Surface Pro 4 because he enjoys the workflow of drawing directly on the screen. The parts of the process that he enjoys most are looking for an idea and creating the final piece. Miguel always has a tiny notebook ready in his pocket, in which he can take down every bit of inspiration whenever he finds something interesting during his walks, journeys, or reading.

"I Am an Earthling" is an illustration celebrating Marlena Agency's (an artist agent) 25th birthday, which shows the supposed role that humans will play in the universe.

"Art Thief" reveals the issue of art theft. It points out the urgency of setting up the strong art insurance system to protect artists' creative works.

"Custom Made" highlights how important it is for a brand to modify and improve its product based on a customer's taste.

"I Want You to Be" is an illustration for *Difusión* that shows that parents and role models are unaware of how much they are affecting children's futures.

3. Prosperity
4. I Want You to Be
5. Memoirs

▲ 2. Customer Trust
▲ 3. Overbooking in Health Care System
▼ 4. Waiting for You

"Viral Promotion" conveys a
message of how to promote
oneself using viral techniques.

"Waiting for You" is a self-
promotional postcard
illustration dedicated to the
celebration of Valentine's Day.

I focus on people and imagine stories inspired by different characters. My colorful and expressive illustrations play with a subtle sense of humor to highlight the fact that life should be fun.

Cinta Arribas

Cinta Arribas is an illustrator who lives and works in Madrid, Spain; she has a BA in Fine Arts from the University of Salamanca in Spain. Cinta enjoys telling stories through her art. Her work is fresh and optimistic, yet perceptive and contemporary. Her ability to simplify shapes and the energy of her characters' poses and gestures are magnetic.

Most of her works start from quick and random sketches. Then she picks the best ones and scans them on a computer or Wacom tablet to add more colors and details using Photoshop. Traveling, urban tribes, flamenco music, and tacky things are the sources of her inspiration.

"Guerrilla Girls" celebrates a group of female artists who campaigned for women's rights in art during the 1980s in New York. Cinta shows the art of criticism, humor, and irony by creating female characters with male traits, like wearing King Kong masks, to imply male dominance.

▲ Guerrilla

"The Expat Pride" portrays the pride of some expat people, who find themselves superior to others when returning home.

"Expats Meeting" shows how Spaniards living abroad have their social meetings. The spanish omelet, red wine, and dance symbolize the nation's culture that is deeply rooted in its people.

▲ 3. Expats Meeting
▶ 4. Bikes

▲ 1. Life on Mars

"Life on Mars" is a song by David Bowie. Impressed by David Bowie's crazy imagination, Cinta has created this work for a tribute exhibition held by Piñata Productions + Perrogato Estudio Creativo.

"Looking for Harmony" was created for *Cambio 16* magazine, a major publication in Spain. It illustrates the fact that the quest of happiness from outside ourselves can obscure what truly lies within us. To be happy, one has to love oneself first.

"Brexit" is featured on 0034 Código Expat, a website aimed at Spanish expats around the world. It reflects the historic referendum in the UK in which the British people dramatically voted for a British exit from the European Union.

▸ 2. Looking for Harmony
▾ 3. Brexit

I would describe my work as classic conceptual illustration. I always try to focus on the concept and use composition, colors, lights, and shadows to make it as clear as possible. I like surprising the viewer and playing with our viewing habits.

Stephan Schmitz

Stephan Schmitz is a conceptual, award-winning illustrator based in Zürich, Switzerland. He loves to surprise his audience, and in a single image, he can tell a whole story through the use of his smart concepts. Stephan started drawing when he was about 7 years old. At that time, he was totally in love with Disney Comics and with some Belgian works like *Spirou*, the *Marsupilami* series, and others following in the footsteps of Hergé. So he started drawing his own stories with the characters of his favorite comic books.

Stephan studied Illustration at Lucerne University of Applied Sciences and Arts. After finishing his studies, he felt a bit lost, as he had not yet found his own style or visual language, so he spent lots of time creating illustrations. It took him about four years to put together a decent portfolio—a series of single images that he thought were good enough to send out to art directors—in order to get more commissions. In the end, it turned out that his effort had paid off as more and more work commissions came in. His work has since been recognized by the Society of Illustrators in New York, American Illustration, *Applied Arts Magazine,* and 3x3 Annual of Contemporary Illustration. In 2015, *Creative Quarterly* mentioned him as one of their top 25 illustrators, and the *Lürzer's Archive* listed him as one of the 200 Best Illustrators Worldwide in 2016/17.

Stephan always looks at what is going on in the field of illustration, how other illustrators interpret different topics, what images they use, and how they tell stories. He loves riding the bus in Zürich and observing the people around, taking screenshots of scenes in movies whenever he notices a nice camera angle, interesting compositions, or a fascinating color palette.

"Breaking the Habit" is an illustration for an
article about how to change one's eating habits.

▲ 1. The Mark and the Void

"The Mark and the Void" is for the book review by the same name written by Paul Murray for *The New York Times*. The story is about a banker and his encounter with an impostor.

"Famous Through Internet" illustrates the phenomenon of young people getting famous via the Internet by using blogs and other social media.

▲ 2. Famous Through Internet

▶ 3. Are You Scared Yet?

"What's to Come" is an illustration for an article about what people can expect financially for the coming year.

I consider my work as "hand-drawn vector art" or "sloppy vector art." I sit between two camps, using the tools (vector, flat color) that are usually applied to more geometric designs to make work that is more loose and sketchy.

Chi Birmingham

Chi Birmingham is a Brooklyn-based illustrator. Originally, he went to school for painting and drawing and developed a kind of a snobby attitude towards illustration. "When I was making art with a capital 'A,' I felt that I had to be a little smarter than I was naturally, and I would avoid a lot of my impulses to make things that were more goofy or cartoonish," said Chi. But eventually, because of all those self-imposed rules that had made art such a chore, he got totally burnt out. It took him seven years to finally realize what he really wanted to make, and by then he was ready to throw in the towel, as he said to himself: "If I'm not making anything serious anyway, why don't I at least try to have some fun." From that point on, he tried to come up with little characters and stories, which later led him naturally to illustration. Currently he works with clients

including *The New Yorker, The New York Times, Bloomberg Businessweek*, and others.

Chi has been a fan of Adobe Flash for about five years, as it lends itself to hand drawing yet makes it very easy and intuitive to give things a flat art style. To draw on the computer he uses a Wacom tablet. Generally he starts his sketches in notebooks to lay out the basic idea and gesture, and leaves all the rendering for the digital stage. He always keeps sketchbooks on hand to write down ideas as they come naturally. "The best method I've found is to set some sort of daily minimum for ideas, say five. I think if you 'honor' really bizarre or dumb ideas, your brain rewards you with the slightly less dumb ones," said Chi.

▲ The Shredder in Me Recognizes the Shredder in You

At the beginning of 2016, Chi made a series of illustrations to put himself in a good mood. This illustration is part of the series, which shows the type of energy that he wants to put in his work.

▲ 1. The Green Printers
▼ 2. Watermelon Man

"The Green Printers" is an advertisement for Jak Prints, a company that plants a tree for every print order.

"Watermelon Man" was commissioned for an article about a town that combined a Watermelon Festival with an antique car show.

I prefer shaky perspectives, differences in proportion, naive compositions, and so on. I am attracted by drawings that are not completely mastered but in which we can feel the sincerity of the illustrator.

Patrick Doyon

Patrick Doyon is an Academy Award-nominated director based in Montreal, Canada. His first professional film, *Sunday* (2011), produced by the National Film Board of Canada, garnered honors on the international festival circuit and was being nominated for an Oscar for best animated short in 2012. Patrick studied Graphic Design at Université du Québec à Montréal and since 2005, he has been splitting his time between illustration and animation. His illustrations for different magazines have won many awards. In 2015, he received the prestigious Governor General's Literary Awards for his illustration of the children's book *The Sandwich Thief* (written by André Marois). Also, he has participated in various projects as a storyboard designer and artistic designer.

When he was young, Patrick used to play a lot of NES (Nintendo Entertainment System) games.

But he was forbidden to play during the week days. So during the week, he spent a lot of time analyzing instruction booklets and reading specialized magazines that were generally well illustrated. He took pleasure imitating the drawings inside the books, and since the games were very pixelated, it allowed him to develop his imagination and will to tell stories.

Since he became a father a few years ago, Patrick has been very interested in children's literature. This is his main source of inspiration at the moment. He loves hanging out in the youth sections of the library to find some inspiration for his graphic style. "There is a profusion of strong graphic universes and a poetic power in this field that I don't find in many other artistic domains," Patrick says.

Since the age of industrialization, human beings have threatened the delicate balance of ecosystems and undermined the survival of species. The collection of "MICROFICHES: Threats on Wildlife" includes 12 illustrations, which reveal that without drastic action, the major human activities may cause serious consequences for nature.

"The Sisters Brothers" is a series of 3 illustrations inspired by the book by the same name written by Patrick deWitt. The story is about the narrator, Eli Sisters, and his brothers who are assassins; they were sent by their fearsome boss to kill Hermann Kermit Warm, an ingenious and likable man. The story is widely viewed as a dark comedy.

My style is simple and based on geometric shapes. I try to use few colors, but they are bright: red, blue, white, turquoise. Also, I like to introduce small touches of humor in my illustrations so that they can appeal to both children and adults.

Teresa Bellon

Teresa Bellon lives in Madrid and works as a professional illustrator. Drawing has been one of Teresa's favorite hobbies since she was a little girl. At the age of 25, she graduated with a degree in Art History, but she was a little confused about what she was supposed to do with her life until she found the answer at Escuela de Arte 10 in Madrid. There she studied illustration and then went on to study graphic design at ESAD in Matosinhos, Portugal. From that moment on she took her drawings more seriously and has been working as a freelance illustrator since 2012. She has participated in several projects and exhibitions and has collaborated with many online stores. Teresa says she feels lucky to work on her own as an illustrator.

Usually Teresa finds her inspiration on the Internet. Aside from that, she finds that traveling, visiting exhibitions, spending some time in nature, reading novels, listening to folk music, attending illustration and design conferences, and watching animals can also be ways for her to find the muse of creation.

MY SURVIVAL KIT.

▴ Survival Kit

"Inktober 2014" is a series of ink drawings that Teresa Bellon created for a project called Inktober. She was asked to make a drawing each day during the month of October. The pieces all had the same style with reduced ranges of colors, simple compositions, and a touch of naiveté and humor.

I LiKE YOU.
YOU ARE WEiRd.
LiKE ME.

▲ 1. Like Me
▼ 2. Brown Sugar
▼ 3. Halloween Pictures

nice to meet you...

LEt ME intROduce YOu
tO "BROWN SUgAR"

Oh PLEASE,
dOn't LEAVE ME!

WE'LL ALWAYS HAVE
OUR HALLOWEEN PiCtURES,
hOnEY.

▲ 4. Sayonara Baby
▼ 5. True Love

This collection is called "Waiting. " Each work illustrates a unique story: a woman carries Death in her dress, a man plays football in the Far West, a girl tries to capture a cloud... Teresa combines scanned old pictures and different textures to create these quirky characters that respond tacitly to her unique style.

▶ 1. Death
▼ 2. Far West
▼ 3. Cloud

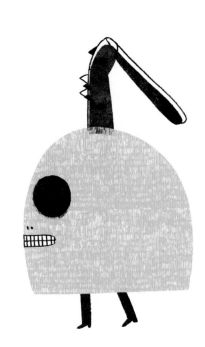

▲ 4. Splash   ▲ 5. Universe
▼ 6. Home   ▼ 7. Mermaid

I pack maximum happiness in my drawings, and when I run out of space I capture the rest in rhyme. It's like children's books for adults. If my art can make someone smile or laugh then I have succeeded, as that is my goal.

Junkyard Sam

Junkyard Sam is a Seattle-based videogame artist and illustrator. He received a full scholarship to the Art Institute of Dallas where he studied computer animation and multimedia production. Since 1995, he has pursued a career as an artist in the videogame industry. For Sam, illustration is a chance to have more control over his work and execute each piece with minimal compromise aside from adapting to a client's needs.

By night he escapes the cold rain by drawing happy worlds full of little yellow peeps, amorous ghosts, and timid monsters with delicate details. Inspired by his kids, Sam's work is infused with a sense of fun. "Kids have little regard for tradition or rules and lack consideration for what others might think of their work. There's a purity to this approach."

▲ All Sun, No Storm

The aliens have landed again but that's okay.
They'll take the fisherman's bait and then go happily on their way.
A man in the window lost his dog but sees him at that car.
He's hoping his dog won't join that pack and travel very far!
In the alley a man with a knife is threatening the birds in the garage,
While the fisherman in pink is happy but missing his entourage.
On days like this in the city when the sun is shining so warm,
Everyone comes out to play to celebrate that there is no storm!

▲ 1. Atari 2600

In 1981 I got this little box of fun,
From my father to his son: my future had begun.
Gripping joystick in my hand, I knew I was the guy,
Born to save the land from the missiles in the sky!

And in Pitfall? I answered Harry's call,
To help him get away from scorpions and rolling logs.
Now I didn't get the patch... But still I grew attached,
Yes the screen was full of blocks and falling barrels Kong dispatched.

But Donkey Kong met his match when I made it to the top,
And I rocked the highest score with the princess that I got!
Now these memories must endure—so I promise Pac-Man ghosts,
Will have a place forever in every drawing that I post!

▲ 2. Getting Fit at the Beach

When a man rides a dog and wears a black flag shirt,
You know he might get in a fight but his dog's not getting hurt.
This punk is getting old and now he's got somewhat a belly,
Because he's working too much and too much time in front the tele.

So he hops up on his beast and rides her down onto the beach,
To see Jessie and her boys and where the Get FIT coach will teach,
How we each can shake it in the water to Get FIT or row the boat,
Instead of sitting round and eating so much food that we explode!

Spontaneous, playful, contemporary, simple, graphic, cartooning- and storytelling-like.

Federica Del Proposto

Born in Rome, Italy, Federica Del Proposto grew up in a medical family, but she was always interested in something else—drawing. When she was a child, drawing was her favorite game— she even drew her own toys. Though she was passionate about drawing, she did not want to go to art school because she regarded herself as a very rebellious teenager. For her, classic Italian art schools were too old-fashioned, so she chose to study architecture. She worked as an intern architect for many years, while publishing her early drawings, mostly comics, by collaborating with some Italian and international publishers. She continued to work as an architect until 2013 when she finally decided to become a professional illustrator. "Drawing was my favorite

game as a child. But it took me a few decades to refine it," Federica says. Currently she lives in Paris and Milan, and she works with clients that include *The Wall Street Journal, The New York Times, Le Figaro, ELLE France,* and others.

Her favorite tools are pencils and fine-liners. She mostly uses Derwent or Faber-Castell colored pencils and Stabilo fine-liners, as she finds lots of fun with the traditional drawing process. Inspired by urban stories, manga, architecture, design, fashion, pop culture, and classic literature, Federica absorbs the things that she has met and seen, and depicts everyday life in her own style with simple lines and soft colors.

▲ Tennis Olympics

"Tennis Olympics" is an illustration for *Illustri Festival*.

▲ 1. Overconsuming

"Overconsuming" is an illustration for *Marie France* magazine.

"Voyage in Portugal" is a series of illustrations for *Les Echos Week-End*. Federica portrays the scenes of Portugal.

▲ 2. Voyage in Portugal 1
▲ 3. Voyage in Portugal 2

A deep fascination for fairy tales, surreal and childhood experiences, among other things, finds their way into my work.

Sveta Dorosheva

Originally from Ukraine and currently based in Israel, Sveta Dorosheva works in the areas of narrative illustration, editorial illustration, and art for books. Sveta has been drawing since childhood. She used to work in the field of creative advertising, but she left and went into illustration when she realized that she had no time for drawing. She evolved as a self-taught artist and has primarily worked on book illustrations and art for magazines as well as brands. Sveta creates hand-drawn illustrations on paper and merges a lot of mythical motifs with her own contemporary ideas.

Mostly she uses ink for the graphics and watercolor for the color. She always researches the project that she is working on and spends lots of time in online museums to learn from the past. Above all, she deems life to be the best source of inspiration.

▲ Boy

"Boy" is a watercolor illustration for *Baku* magazine in Azerbaijan, in which Sveta narrated the childhood memories of a celebrity, who grew up in Baku. Detailed fragments flow out from his hat and become his memory of this city, a place for lost-and-found.

▲ 1. Childhood: Water
▲ 2. Childhood: Pillow Fight
◄ 3. Childhood: Pillow Fight (Details)

"Childhood" is a collection of ink illustrations for a book entitled *How to Handle a Child* that captures some memorable moments and scenes of childhood.

▲ 4. Childhood: School

▲ 1. Childhood: Drawing
▲ 2. Childhood: Ladybugs
▲ 3. Childhood: Reading
▲ 4. Childhood: Seaside

I try to keep my illustrations honest and humble, with an undertone of activism. Being kind to animals and the environment is a very important part of my vision.

Lieke van der Vorst

Lieke van der Vorst always wants to make a positive impact on the world, and illustration seems to be the natural path to achieve this. Lieke grew up in Kaatsheuvel, a small town in the Netherlands; every summer her parents would pack up their De Waard tent and drive 13 hours to Provence in France to camp among the lavender fields. Being close to nature has greatly influenced her life and work. In the summer of 2011, Lieke started Liekeland to share her illustrations online. From her studio in Eindhoven, the Netherlands, she illustrates her prints and commissioned work. She tries to make illustrations with stories about gardening, food, and the love for animals.

Soft colored pencils are Lieke's favorite tools. Apart from colored pencils, she uses graphite pencils, ballpoint pens, and digital tools like Photoshop. She finds inspiration from almost everything—cookbooks, food, farmers' markets, stories from friends, documentaries, books, nature, and daily encounters.

▲ Bont voor Dieren

"Bont voor Dieren" features a woman hugging a raccoon. It is for an organization of the same name that fights against the use of animal fur, especially from the raccoon, whose fur is usually used for coats.

"Flow" features a woman on a bike with her dog who has just come back from the market.

"Piet Hein Eek" illustrates the workspace of the designer by the same name.

"Pompoen" depicts a story about three animals having a great Christmas night with Indian curry. The forested backdrop is created using a linocut technique.

▲ 1. Flow
▼ 2. Birds

▲ 3. Piet Hein Eek
▶ 4. Pompoen

x

▲ 3. Piet Hein Eek
▶ 4. Pompoen

Lieke creates "Moestuin" in memory of her grandmother's house with a vegetable garden in front where her mother used to work.

"*Flow* Magazine Gardening" is an illustration for *Flow* magazine about Lieke's own garden, where she has planted many pumpkins and a lot of flowers.

"Oogstfeest" portrays friends having dinner together in their garden.

▲ 1. Moestuin
▶ 2. *Flow* Magazine Gardening

▲ 3. Moestuin (Details)
▲ 4. *Flow* Magazine Gardening (Details)
▼ 5. Oogstfeest

My work is mainly focused on character design and detailed self-contained compositions.

Marija Tiurina

Marija Tiurina is an illustrator based in London. She moved to the UK from Eastern Europe and studied multimedia technology and design at Brunel University. She has worked as a full-time concept illustrator and games artist in a central London-based studio since she graduated from university in 2013. Currently she spends half the week working as a freelance illustrator for an East London-based customized children's book studio. She dedicates the rest of her time to her own personal projects as much as possible.

▲ Morra (The Moomins)

Marija Tiurina calls this series "Small Drawings." She enjoys looking for inspiration from daily moments and reproduces the scenes using pencil, ink, and watercolor. Each character under her pen is like a small universe.

▲ 1. Harakiri

▲ 2. Puglife
▲ 3. Wednesday
▶ 4. Sharing Is Caring

My mysterious and conceptual illustrations, often depicting characters in surreal situations, are rich in detail and color.

Helena Perez Garcia

Helena Perez Garcia is a Spanish illustrator and graphic designer based in London. She obtained a degree in Fine Arts in Sevilla in 2005. She then moved to Valencia and worked on a Master's degree in Design and Illustration. In 2012, she relocated to London where she is currently based. She has published two illustrated books in France, *Louna au Musée* and *Bonne Nuit Louna*. Among her clients are publishing houses like Penguin Random House, Anaya, and Santillana. She also regularly collaborates with magazines and other publications.

Helena always wanted to be a graphic designer because she aspired to work in the creative industry. Later she found that illustrating gave her more freedom and was much closer to art than graphic design. Thus she focuses more on illustration and expressing herself through images. She mostly uses gouache and adds details using pencils and pastels, as she loves the flatness of color. Her work is inspired by art, most recently by Italian art after her visit to Rome a few months ago. Also she sources inspiration from literature and philosophy, especially the works and ideas of Albert Camus, one of her favorite authors.

1. Through the Night
2. The Wall
3. Bay Leaves
4. The Bully Project Mural

"Through the Night" is an illustration that Helena created for her solo exhibition, "On The Other Side," at Ó! Gallery held in Lisbon in 2016. A girl is about to hide in a bush in the middle of the night. What is driving her to do so?

"The Wall" and "Bay Leaves" are personal illustrations showing girls who hide part of their body or face from the outside world without a readable expression on their face. No one knows their reason for hiding. Is it coincident or on purpose? Is it an action of escaping or merging?

"The Bully" is an illustration for the Bully Project Mural launched by Adobe. The project talks about bullying and its consequences.

▲ 2. The Mirror
▸ 3. Tea Party

"The Jungle" tells of a brave girl wandering through the jungle in the company of her loyal friend, the tiger.

"The Mirror" and "Tea Party" are illustrations from Helena's solo exhibition "On The Other Side" at Ó! Gallery in Lisbon in 2016.

I try to capture the lovely interactions between nature and humans in a familiar, yet respectful way.

Sehee Chae

Sehee Chae is a Korean illustrator. She has been telling stories through pictures for as long as she can remember. Drawing is always the way that she visualizes and communicates with the world. She is interested in expressing the fictional worlds based on her favorite music, lyrics, movies and so on. And she finds that illustration is a perfect way to outline the backdrop, character, and story. She enjoys working with traditional painting methods and materials like pencils, oil pastels, and digital tools like Photoshop. Her work has been featured in newsletters, magazines, book covers, and more.

▲ In the Space

What if we perform various activities on a space ship? It would be more amusing than what is shown in the painting.

"A Day of the Girl" is a story about the warmth of the sky during sunset, and about loneliness.

In "The Journey of the Girls," the cold, desolate winter was close at hand, and four girls were setting out for their mysterious and appealing journey into the unknown.

▲ 2. A Girl, A Cat, A Butterfly and...
▲ 3. The Journey of the Girls

▲ 1. The Garden of Silence
▲ 2. Liar Liar
▲ 3. The Christmas in Summer

"The Garden of Silence" depicts a Korean girl stepping into a tropical botanical garden where she finds African birds with fancy feathers and plants she has never seen before.

"Liar Liar" is an illustration designed for the third mini album cover of Oh My Girl, a Korean K-pop girl band. "Liar Liar" is the name of a song included on the album.

"The Christmas in Summer" portrays two girls from the north spending their winter in exotic Southeast Asia. The trip is extraordinary to them, as if they are having Christmas Day in the peaceful summer.

I want my illustrations to be simple and I normally try to keep my compositions clean, bold, and easily readable, using as few elements as possible.

Raúl Soria

Raúl Soria is a Spanish-born, Berlin-based illustrator. He received his degree in Visual Communication from Berlin University of the Arts in 2013 and has since been freelancing, mainly producing images for various newspapers and magazines. His clients include Mercedes-Benz Next, *Variety,* De Correspondent, *FOCUS,* Babbel, and *La Maleta de Portbou*, among others.

Raúl says that being an illustrator is a way of escaping a life that he was not enjoying. After he graduated from high school in Zaragoza, the creative world was not an option for him. Artists were something that he heard about from TV or magazines, but they did not belong to his neighborhood. In his adolescence, he was told to study something that would assure him job opportunities in the future, and he just followed this advice and got a degree in Tourism Management. After that, he worked as a waiter under pretty bad conditions, partied a lot, and became quite unsatisfied with everything. During those years he stopped drawing completely. Later, he moved to Berlin, when his life began to change. In Berlin, he suddenly found that he was surrounded by musicians, designers, and

creatives of all kinds. He got a chance to share a flat with three students majoring in design. They taught him a lot of things and encouraged him to apply to a design school. Eventually he did, and it all worked out fine.

The first two years of freelancing were quite horrible: few clients, lots of badly paid or unpaid jobs, much stress, little money... but fortunately, things started to get better as he moved on.

Raúl values simple compositions, but he is rather flexible in this sense, and he also loves the details. It all depends on what he is doing and for what concrete purpose. "Illustrations are functional," says Raúl. Also, he always seeks some kind of "aha!" effect, and he wants his work to somehow have a soul. For example, he finds it quite lovely when his work makes people smile. "Summing it all up in one sentence, what I try to achieve in my work is a balanced combination of communicativeness, simplicity, and charm—the measure of each varying from piece to piece, depending on its purpose."

▲ Rookies Try New Ways to Standout

This editorial illustration for *Variety* tells a story
about how new shows and networks were
campaigning hard to get into the Emmy race.

"Jeans" and "Disaster" are illustrations for an article that explains the etymological origin of some English words. "The word 'jeans' is likely derived from the name of the city 'Genoa' in Italy where jeans were first produced. Sailors in Northern Italy were exporting jeans from as far back as the 17th Century." "The English word 'disaster' dates back to the Old Italian 'disastro' derived from Greek. The pejorative prefix 'dis-' and 'aster'(star) can be interpreted as 'bad star,' or an ill-starred event."

"The Brickmasters in the Shadows" is an illustration for an article about funds and big international banks shaking the market with enormous investments, above all, in social housing sectors.

▲ 1. An Introduction to Etymology: Jeans
▼ 2. An Introduction to Etymology: Disaster

▲ 3. Comfort
▼ 4. The Brickmasters in the Shadows

▲ The Difficulties of the Love Choice

"The Difficulties of the Love Choice" is an editorial illustration for an article narrating the fact that in virtual social networks, people are suffering from the difficulties of making choices about things that they really need and love.

I love using bright and vintage colors and keeping an isometric view. It is my favorite perspective because in this way I can show every element of the image as clearly as possible.

Andrea De Santis

Born in Brescia, Italy, Andrea De Santis has been a creative person since he was a child. He has worked for many years as a graphic designer at a variety of companies in different fields such as toys and apparel, but illustration has always been his real love. Currently he works as a freelancer collaborating with many important magazines and publishers based in the United States, the United Kingdom, Germany, and others. His clients include *O, The Oprah Magazine*, *WWD*, *Redbook*, *Real Simple*, *Die Zeit*, *Psychologies* magazine, Macmillan Publishers, and so on. He usually sketches his ideas and then works with Adobe Illustrator to make detailed elements. Then he goes on to use Photoshop to add textures and shadows. Andrea mostly scouts inspiration from the Internet and reality; he says, "Combining a simple object and its function can be both useful and a perfect mix for a great illustration."

"The Creative House" is a collective project. Artists from all over the world present an interpretation of a creative house—a place for art, inspiration, and excellence. This is Andrea's vision.

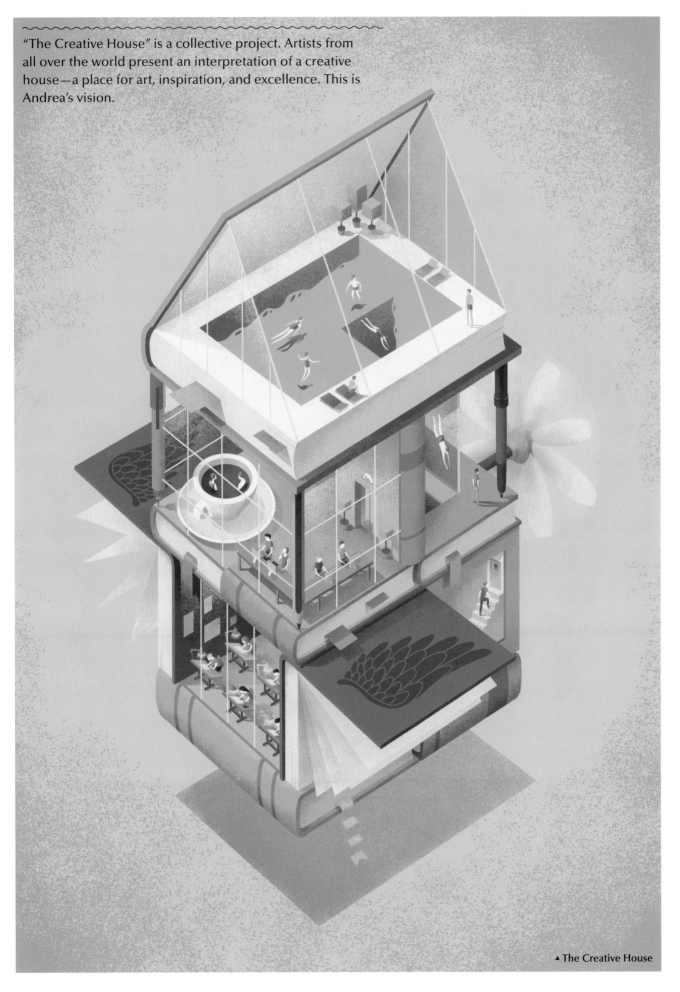

▲ The Creative House

These are examples from a series of illustrations for a 2017 calendar. They record the most wonderful scenic spots at Lake Garda in northern Italy.

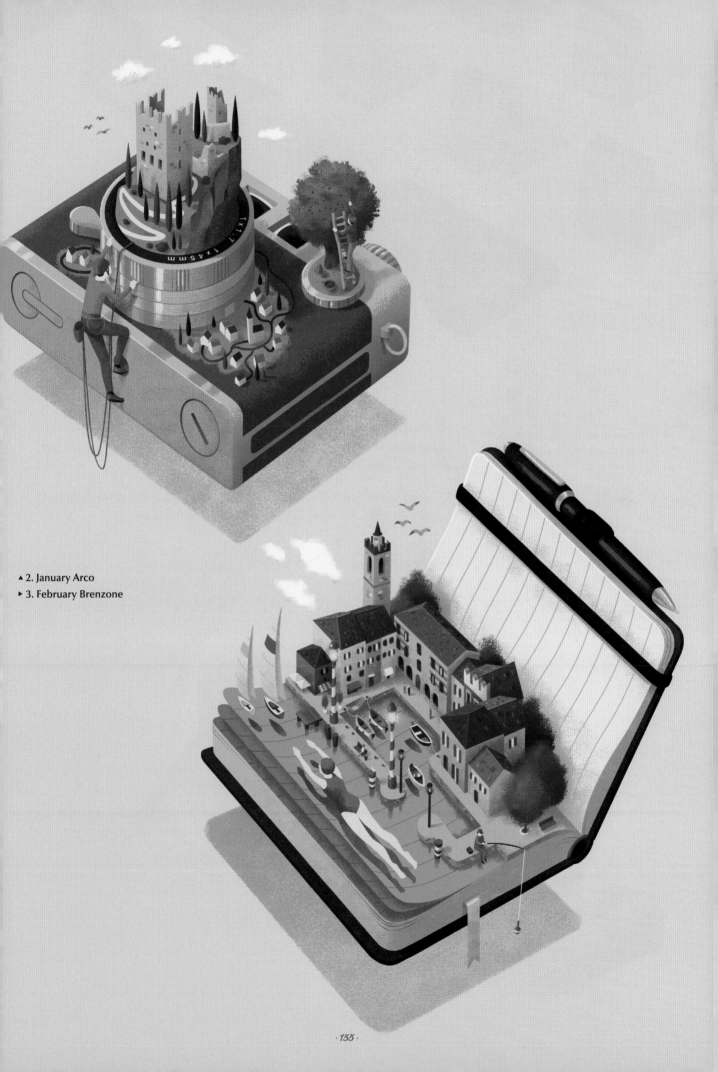

▲ 2. January Arco
► 3. February Brenzone

▲ 1. Illustration for *Psychologies* 1
▼ 2. Illustration for *Psychologies* 2

Illustration for *Psychologies* 1 is based on a woman suffering from her growing debts and Ostrich Syndrome.

Illustration for *Psychologies* 2 is based on an article titled "My Job Is All Important" about a woman who is too tied to her work.

▶ 3. Go and Listen
▼ 4. How to Save Time for *Reebok* magazine
▼ 5. Holiday for *WWD* magazine

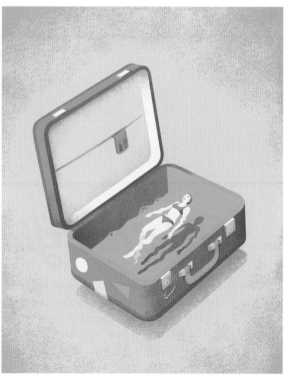

I translate aestheticism into my work by mixing curves of wobbly geometry with a lighter pattern of pastel colors, which together come to life as a texture.

Tristan Gion

Tristan Gion is a freelance illustrator based in France. He has always been fascinated by drawing, especially drawings that tell small stories. He likes to draw inspiration from the world around him. With his simple to almost childish themes, he always tries to give a utopian poetic vision to his work. He works with Photoshop as well as a tablet. From time to time, he makes hand-drawn paintings or uses watercolor to give varied textures to purely digital illustrations.

"Amor" is a collection of true stories of sex. Tristan has conversed with many people, including his friends, on the topic of intimacy. He then reinterprets their intimate stories in a poetic way.

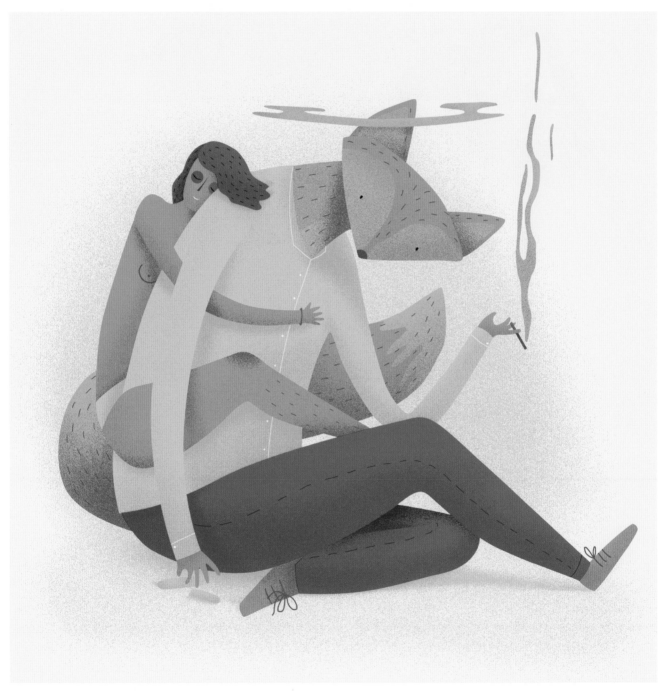

▲ Amor: Calin

▴ 1. Amor: Wrap
▴ 2. Amor: Flan

▲ 3. Amor: Train
▼ 4. Amor: Pierce
▼ 5. Amor: Pecuv

PIERCING

▲ 1. Matin Ordinaire 1
▲ 2. Matin Ordinaire 2
▼ 3. Matin Ordinaire 3

Although banalized by the name, "Matin Ordinaire" is an extraordinary fairytale-like collection. The cue of this collection is derived from a simple two-person game, Le Cadavre Exquis. One person is asked to draw one part of his/her dream house; the other person should continue the drawing without looking at what has already been drawn. The rest of the drawings are made in the same fashion. So the collection ends up with a mixture of forms and ideas.

"Petite Joubarbe" is the name of a small mountain flower. The series tells a story of holidays, anecdotes, and events that occurred during a trip in the mountains alone.

▲ 4. Petite Joubarbe 1
▼ 5. Petite Joubarbe 2
▼ 6. Petite Joubarbe 3

Solid colors and bold geometric shapes with exaggerated proportions are the constant elements in my work.

Tiago Galo

Tiago Galo is a Portuguese illustrator based in Lisbon. He worked exclusively as an architect for ten years. But this work turned out to be such an intense and overwhelming experience that it left him no time to do anything else. "When I started studying the Bauhaus movement, in which painting, design, and architecture were getting influenced by one another, I got the message that I could still get myself involved with all of them," said Tiago. So when he realized that he was not happy as an architect, he started to work as an illustrator by collaborating with small fanzines and exhibitions. Influenced by both cinema and comics, especially the ones by Wes Anderson, Jim Jarmusch, or Buster Keaton, he adds unconventional and sometimes surreal twists to all his illustrations. However, reality is always his source of ideas. "I am always getting odd ideas in the most common places and everyday situations. I tend to observe people everywhere I go and I am always coming up with stories in my head, like imagining how that guy got the stain on his shirt, or at which subway station the middle-age couple will get off."

An illustration for the "After the Volcano" exhibition held at the Walk & Talk Arts Festival in the Azores.

▲ Lava People

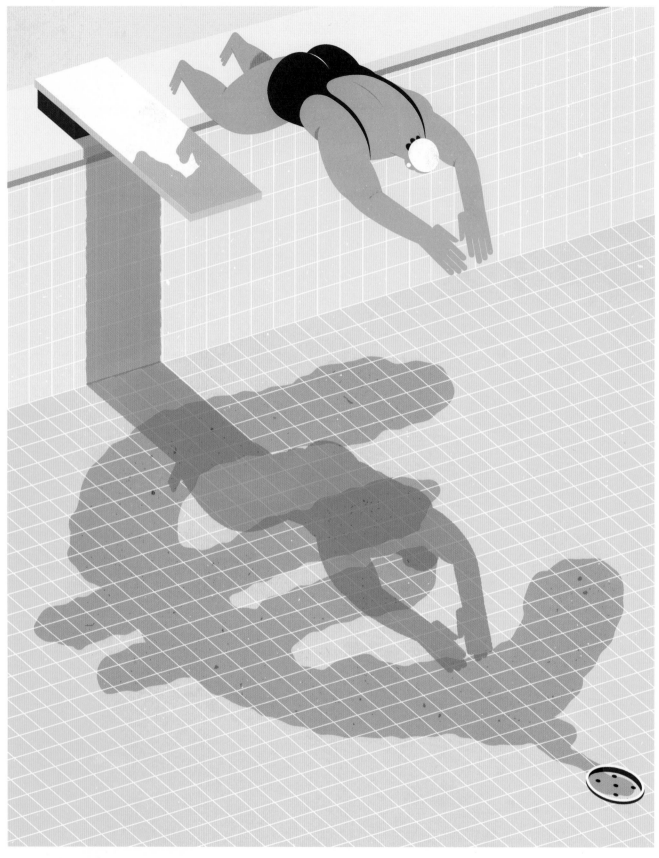

▲ 1. Down the Drain

"Down the Drain" is an illustration for *DATUM* magazine about Austrian public bathing lidos and how they are financial disasters.

"Caught Two" and "Wrong Kind of People" are illustrations for the "People Are Strange" exhibition at the LX Factory in Lisbon.

▸ 2. Caught Two
▾ 3. Wrong Kind of People

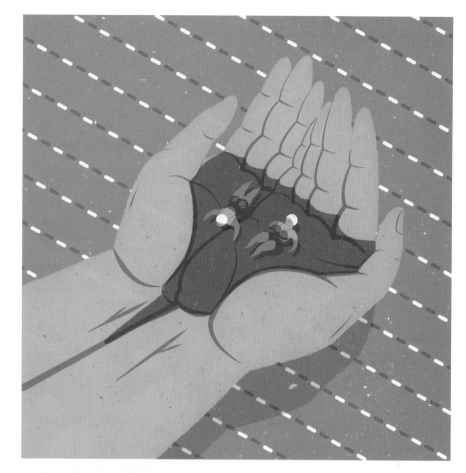

▲ 1. Wild Guess
▼ 2. Wasted
▼ 3. Keep It Dry

◄ 4. What You See
▼ 5. Introvert

◄ 4. What You See

Naive. I've always liked that word. I remember learning about it for the first time while I was discovering the work of Rousseau and I think it is a good fit for my work too. I like the playful aspect of my illustrations, the strokes of the pencil that remind me of children's drawings and the freedom of creation.

Eleonora Arosio

Eleonora Arosio is an Italian illustrator based in Milan and wherever else she travels. Born in 1992, she started being passionate about drawing from an early age. All of her teachers confirmed what her mother already knew: "She is going to become an artist!" When she went to university, she was often asked to focus more on contemporary art. But Eleonora knew that she just wanted to grab a piece of paper and draw something beautiful, something that she liked, without too many whys and hows. "That was the moment I figured out illustration was my path," she says. After graduating from NABA Academy in Milan, she started dedicating herself to illustrations and depicting the ironic issues of everyday life from a woman's point of view. "I think I am part of the new feminism that is trying to remind all girls that we are beautiful; that we are not necessarily someone's halves; and that we can do it," remarks Eleonora.

Like every artist, she takes inspiration from what is around her. Pencils and paper are the materials that Eleonora adores the most. She tends to work with very dense, bold colors. Her idea of illustration is that it has to be eye candy; it has to make the viewer feel good.

▲ It's OK, It's OK, It's OK

"It's OK, It's OK, It's OK" is for those who need
a whole army of ladies telling them "It's OK."

▲ 1. The New Legendary Sea Monsters 1
▲ 2. The New Legendary Sea Monsters 2

This collection was born during a water aerobics class. The idea behind it is that a bunch of ladies moving and burning calories could turn into modern water beasts.

▾ 3. The New Legendary Sea Monsters 3

▲ 1. Slow Legs

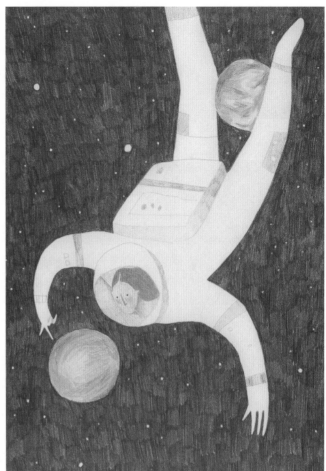

▲ 2. Eva
▲ 3. Hello Kepler!
▼ 4. L'Orticoltore

"Slow Legs" is part of a series of illustrations based on the connections, colors, and calm atmosphere revolving around water.

"Eva" is an illustration for a story by Gaia Rau about a young girl spending her summer time in Italy.

"Hello Kepler!" is a tribute to the discovery of Kepler-452, an exoplanet orbiting the Sun.

Eleonora created "L'Orticoltore" in collaboration with a horticulturist. Plants and nudity are always two graceful themes to join together.

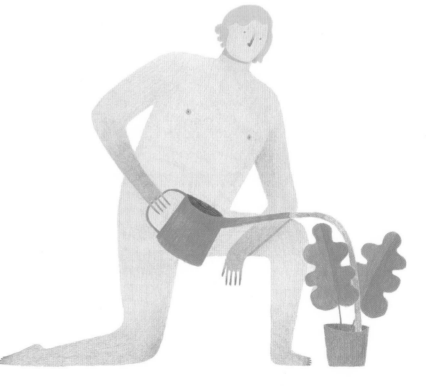

I feel the weight of shapes and volumes. And the color serves to create atmospheres and three-dimensional environments.

Anna Pirolli

Anna Pirolli is an illustrator living and working in Milan. She started drawing at the age of three, because her mother taught art at school. Naturally her mother taught her the basics of design—perspective, color, outline, and so on—and instructed her to look into things critically. At the age of eighteen, she moved to Milan where she attended a three-year course at the European Design Institute. She likes to call herself a "planner" as she is interested in all the steps of the creative process, from the general conception to the tiny details. She tries to make her illustrations colorful worlds in which the viewers can immerse themselves. For more than ten years she has worked with corporations and communication companies. Her clients include Kinder Ferrero, Telecom, MTV, ESPN, Fox, Disney, and so on.

Anna mainly works with Photoshop and is now experimenting with acrylic colors, pencils, and oils. She believes that small and hidden things often inspire great ideas. Nature is a constant element in Anna's illustrations. "I love plants and animals of any kind, so they often have a preponderant role in my stories."

▲ The Charm of Creation: Mental Peace

▲ 1. The Charm of Creation: Mental Presence

Anna made this collection for an international exhibition of illustrations. The theme for this year was "Protection of the Environment and Care for the Planet as a Common Home to Protect for the Future Generations," which aimed to promote love of and care for the world where we live.

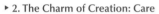

▸ 2. The Charm of Creation: Care
▾ 3. The Charm of Creation: Compassion

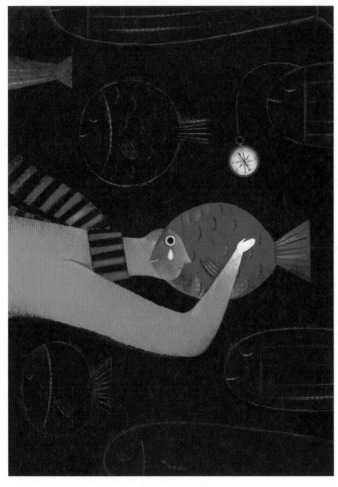

I create graphic works that go straight to the point with much closer perspectives and centralized subjects.

Shout

Born in Pordenone, Italy, in 1977, Shout, aka Alessandro Gottardo, now works and lives in Milan. He studied art in Venice and illustration at the European Design Institute in Milan, Italy. His "Shout" pseudonym was born in 2005; it is a name that represented his idea to speak with his own true voice. Shout's conscious goal was to work on projects in which he could express his personal beliefs about a subject, rather than always being forced to present the safe, commercial option. His client list includes newspapers, magazines, ad brands, design studios, and animation studios. His work has received several international awards. His success followed worldwide recognition and celebration when his work was featured by some important publications, including the Society of Illustrators and the Society of Publication Designers.

▲ Quite America

◄ 1. Brothers
◄ 2. Friendship
▼ 3. Call Me if You Need Me

▲ 4. Turtle

▲ 1. USA at Cannes Festival

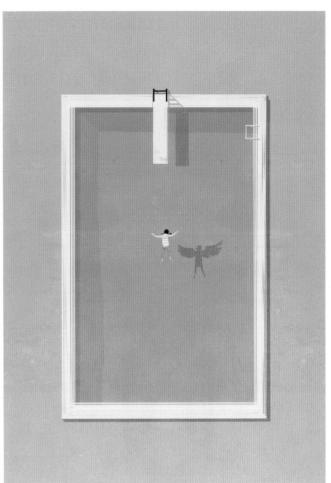

▲ 2. Leisure
▲ 3. Confession
▼ 4. Confession (Details)

I make my work as minimalistic as possible and leave a margin to evoke the audience's imagination.

Taku Bannai

Taku Bannai is a Japanese illustrator based in Tokyo. Taku graduated with a BA in Graphic Design from Tama Art University. He began his profession as an illustrator by collaborating with multiple design advertisement companies. His clients include Japan Airlines, *Japan Post*, Suntory, Isetan, Mini, and many others.

▲ The Sea Which Came with Father

▲ 2. 16.5°c
▲ 3. Winter

These are Taku's personal illustrations. With a simple composition and patches of color, Taku leaves margin in the graphics to make them look like landscapes from afar.

▲ 1. The Sunset
▲ 2. Matasaburo the Wind Imp
▲ 3. Blue Sky

I break down objects, environments, and people into basic shapes and rebuild them with my own interpretation using color, simple lines, and textures.

Jeannie Phan

Jeannie Phan is an award-winning illustrator based in Toronto, Canada, whose work has been published globally. She studied at OCAD University with a major in Illustration. After graduation, she worked in a small gallery in downtown Toronto for a year, from which she got familiar with the local art scene. Then she left to pursue a career as a full-time illustrator.

She is known for using a full spectrum of colors favoring brightness and boldness to evoke some sort of optimism in the colors that she chooses. Although she works primarily with digital tools, she does well in acrylic gouache and watercolor. She tries to combine organic strokes in subtle ways by overlaying transparencies, grainy textures, and imperfect lines.

This illustration is for a book review on Rebecca Hunt's book *Everland*. The author dramatically parallels two separate scientific expeditions in Antarctica that are a hundred years apart.

▲ Everland

▲ 1. Civic Engagement

"Civic Engagement" points out that getting involved in the community in meaningful ways not only leads to a happier life as we age, but can even reverse brain shrinkage.

"Choosing Your Own Reading" raises a question about why there are so many books about death.

▲ 2. Missing Women in Film
▶ 3. Choosing Your Own Reading

▲ 1. Resource Rulers

"Community" is for the 20th anniversary issue of *Bitch* magazine. It portrays the theme of "community" and pays tribute to feminism.

▸ 2. Community
▾ 3. No Point Loving

I use flat yet minimal shapes with a focus on the complexity of human emotion.

Jenn Liv

Jenn Liv, aka Jennifer Liu, is an award-winning Chinese illustrator based in Toronto, Canada, where she studied at OCAD University. The first few years out of school were the most difficult for her. She spent time reinventing her portfolio and tried to discover an artistic voice of her own. Now she gradually gains more attention from the world. In her work, she focuses on flat shapes with an emphasis on bright color and lighting. She also tries to pay attention to objects, moods, or feelings that she wants to convey through her pieces. She enjoys drawing powerful and confident women, especially those in glamorous fashion settings. Occasionally she likes to print things using the risograph technique.

▲ Waste

This image reflects the unnecessary
waste of materials.

▲ 1. Asian Squatting

"Asian Squatting" and "Pizza Girl" are Jenn's personal works, which she created by drawing inspiration from the things she saw in daily life.

"Growth" is an editorial illustration for *PLANSPONSOR*.

▸ 2. Growth
▾ 3. Pizza Girl

Cute and feminine. I enjoy drawing girls and kids. I love to try lots of different things and want to explore a rich variety.

Dung Ho

Dung Ho grew up in Hue, Vietnam, and currently lives and works in HCM, Vietnam. Ever since she was a child, Dung has showed great interest in drawing. Encouraged by her father, she went to art school, which turned out to be a good start. She mainly uses a Wacom tablet and Photoshop for drawing. Her work stands out with its dreamy colors and cute characters.

▲ Yellow Flowers

These illustrations are Dung's daily work. Each piece is a reflection of some moment that she finds interesting and special—it can be a moment when she is listening to a song, watching a movie, or even eating cookies.

▲ 1. Take a Nap
▼ 2. Jane
▼ 3. Naughty Boy

▲ 4. Take a Walk with My Crocodile
▼ 5. The Boy and the Ducks

◄ 1. Fly Away Flowers
▼ 2. Sad Girl

▲ 3. Catch the Stars

I am especially interested in emotions and stories. Many of my pieces may involve elements that are emotionally consistent.

Alice Yu Deng

Alice Yu Deng is an illustrator who is originally from Yangzhou, China. She graduated from Maryland Institute College of Art with a BFA in Illustration. Her work has been featured by the Association of Illustrators, the Society of Illustrators, *3x3 Magazine*, and others. Alice enjoys the process of solving problems both conceptually and visually and has a special interest in narratives and emotional content.

Alice's passion for drawing and painting started at a very young age. Throughout the years, doodling and making images has become a vital part of her life. It was in her second year at college that she realized that she wanted to become an illustrator. For her, illustration is a visual language that communicates ideas and interacts with the world. The process of making illustrations is like building up and developing the language system. On one hand, there are infinite possibilities to explore; on the other hand, the creative process follows a logic that makes the language work in the real world. Alice wants to create things and communicate with people through her art, so she enjoys the process of creating.

▲ Sashimi Land

This image is part of the series "Glimpse of Japan." This one focuses on depicting Japanese food.

▲ 1. The Cat Island

▸ 2. The Curly Beard 1
▾ 3. The Curly Beard 2

"The Cat Island" is part of the series "Glimpse of Japan." It portrays the island in Japan called Tashirojima. On this island, the population of cats is even larger than that of human beings.

"The Curly Beard 1 & 2" are part of the "Chuanqi" series that consists of several short stories from the Tang Dynasty. Alice has created portraits for each of the three main characters.

I prefer apparently ordinary stories, where everything is linked to a fairytale atmosphere. I like the wonder of discovering something new in ordinary things.

Paolo Domeniconi

Paolo Domeniconi lives and works in Spilamberto, Italy. After gaining artistic experience in advertising and through various freelance projects in the 1990s, he became interested in illustrations. Working in digital media, he has illustrated more than 40 books for Italian and international publishers.

The illustration work by Paolo Domeniconi appears almost as though it has been rendered entirely with a set of colored pencils and watercolor paints, but it is actually the result of well-mastered digital media.

▲ Taste the Clouds: Music

Taste the Clouds is a children's book published by Creative Editions, an imprint of The Creative Company (USA). Can you hear color or see music wherever you look? Is it possible to touch the stars or smell a rainbow? Venturing off the beaten path of nonfiction board books, *Taste the Clouds* encourages the youngest readers to expand their imaginations and senses to describe the world around us.

▲ 1. Taste the Clouds: Moon
▲ 2. Taste the Clouds: Stars
▸ 3. Taste the Clouds: Clouds
▸ 4. Taste the Clouds: Rainbow

Did Your Beard Miss Me? is a children's book published by Grimm Press (Taiwan). Little Lita misses her dad when he is away at work. He misses his daughter as well. So, how does Lita's dad miss his little girl? The answers are with his beard which Lita always enjoys rustling against her cheek; with his ears which invariably perk up every time Lita sings; and most of all, with his eyes which will always love seeing Lita's bright, innocent smile.

▲ 1. Did Your Beard Miss Me? 1

▲ 2. Did Your Beard Miss Me? 2

▶ 3. Did Your Beard Miss Me? 3

My work is often described as melancholic, but I like to think that I try to find the place where melancholy and beauty meet. My fascination with narrative means that in my work, I generally try to tell a story or suggest a bigger picture.

Owen Gent

Owen Gent is an award-winning illustrator based in Bristol in the Southwest of England. As well as his own illustration work, Owen writes, illustrates, and directs for Uncle Ginger animation studio, which he runs with Hugh Cowling. With a focus on the metaphorical and the ethereal, Owen's work explores a place where beauty and melancholy exist together. Working largely on book covers, editorial, and self-written narrative projects, his work prefers to hint and suggest a story, leaving interpretation to the audience rather than telling the whole tale.

▲ Your Blissful Shadow

◂ 1. Bankton House
▾ 2. Spatially Literate Experience Design

▲ 3. Noon
▲ 4. Façade
▸ 5. Lovers 2

▲ 1. What Are You Looking For?

▸ 2. What It Means to Be Black and British in Trump's America
▾ 3. Tess of the D'Urbervilles

Romantic colors and realistic issues are the essential elements in my illustrations.

Linshu Zeng

Linshu Zeng, who works as an illustrator, is an idealist and a member of the Shenzhen Graphic Design Association as well. She focuses on translating the issues that everyone might meet in daily life into visual language from which readers can think about the meaning of life. The surreal imagery and compositions come into being in her work to interpret her philosophic thinking and pursuits. Linshu makes her work with digital tools. She likes using fresh colors, choosing surreal ways to describe realistic problems, and showing her philosophic thinking.

▲ Seeing the Happiness

Autumn can leave people immersed in their own thoughts, and "Late Autumn" is about the praise of beautiful things. The autumn is short, but we have to learn how to cherish it.

"Paper Boats" comes from a modern poem of a Chinese poetess. It describes paper boats that could take our memories to someone who we are missing.

▲ 1. Dramatic Changes

▲ 2. Late Autumn
▾ 3. Paper Boats
▾ 4. Who Tied the Bell?

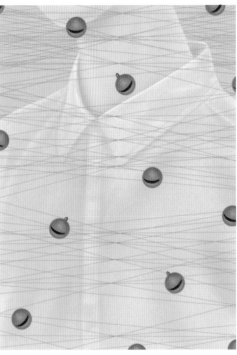

In "Fight with Self," Linshu wants to tell us that we cannot avoid competing or even fighting with ourselves. When we are involved in this kind of state, we feel terrible. However, we need to understand that self-analysis might be a wonderful battle. A person may have different thoughts regarding the same thing—sweet or stressful, open or secret—no matter how it turns out, it is still a normal state that we do not need to evade or be upset about.

▲ 1. Fight with Self
◄ 2. Waiting

▲ 3. Dating
▼ 4. Homesickness

Gentle and happy.

Tina Siuda

Tina Siuda is a Polish illustrator based in Porto, Portugal. She has degrees in Graphic Design and Printing Techniques. She studied in Poland and Portugal and currently works as a freelancer, drawing at home with the help of her cats. Silkscreen is her favorite printing technique and pencil is her favorite tool. Tina likes to experiment with the idea of making something that looks either very tiny or gigantic. She uses mixed media like graphite, color pencils, and colorful paper. There are a lot of textures and shiny details in her illustrations. When it is necessary, she transplants those elements into digital works. Tina always tries to create a gentle and peaceful atmosphere in her illustrations and inhabit them with imaginary friends.

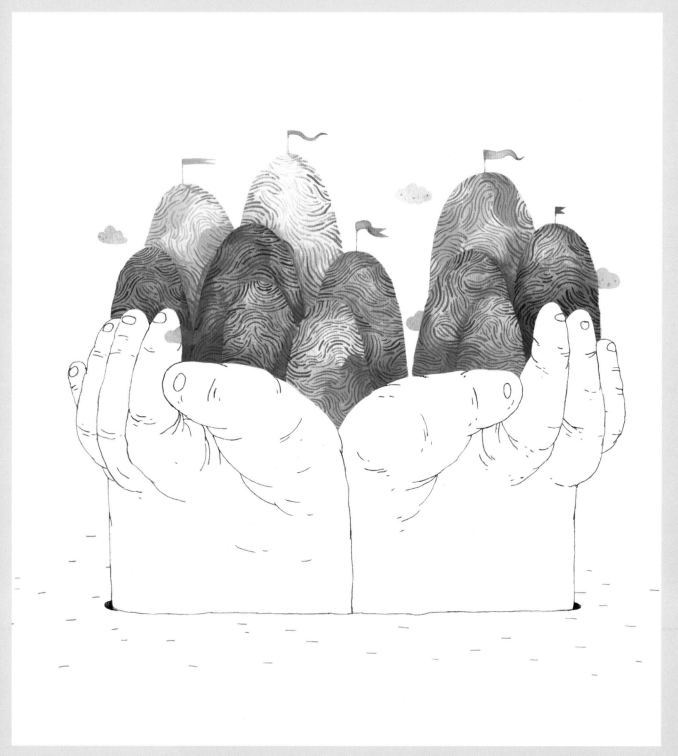

▲ Handful of Mountains

Keep a piece of world for yourself.

A series of illustrations from a self-published book *Little Rock*. It depicts a story about a small rock that goes alone on an adventure and meets a mysterious giant.

▲ 1. Rubik's Cube
▲ 2. Mountain Fingers
▼ 3. A Lake of Tears

Index

Alice Wellinger
www.alice-wellinger.com
Page · 026~033

Alice Yu Deng
aliceyudeng.com
Page · 208~211

Anna Pirolli
www.annapirolli.it
Page · 176~179

Andrea De Santis
www.adesantis.it
Page · 152~157

Chi Birmingham
www.chibirmingham.com
Page · 094~097

Cinta Arribas
www.cintarribas.es
Page · 082~087

Dung Ho
dungho.me
Page · 202~207

Eero Lampinen
www.eerolampinen.com
Page · 050~057

Eleonora Arosio
www.eleonoraarosio.com
Page · 170~175

Federica Del Proposto
www.federicadelproposto.com

Page · 114~117

Helena Perez Garcia
helenaperezgarcia.co.uk

Page · 134~139

Jasu Hu
www.jasuhuart.com

Page · 064~069

Jenn Liv
www.jennliv.com

Page · 198~201

Jeannie Phan
www.jeanniephan.com

Page · 192~197

Jesús Sotés Vicente
www.jesussotes.com

Page · 070~075

Junkyard Sam

junkyardsam.com

Page · 110~113

Kathrin Honesta

www.behance.net/kathrinhonesta

Page · 018~025

Lieke van der Vorst

www.liekeland.nl

Page · 124~129

Linshu Zeng

linshu.strikingly.com

Page · 224~229

Lisk Feng

liskfeng.com

Page · 042~049

Marija Tiurina

marijatiurina.com

Page · 130~133

Massimiliano di Lauro

www.behance.net/massimilianodilauro

Page · 058~063

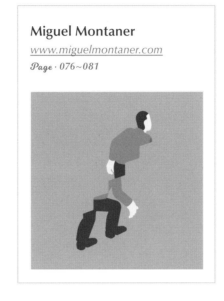

Miguel Montaner

www.miguelmontaner.com

Page · 076~081

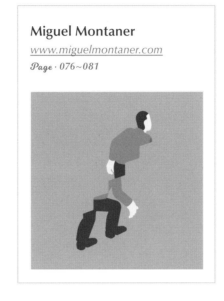

Owen Gent

www.owengent.com

Page · 218~223

Paolo Domeniconi

www.domeniconi.it

Page · 212~217

Patrick Doyon

www.doiion.com

Page · 098~103

Raúl Soria

www.raulsoria.de

Page · 146~151

Ruben Ireland
rubenireland.co.uk
Page · 034~041

Sehee Chae
www.behance.net/seheechae
Page · 140~145

Shout
www.alessandrogottardo.com
Page · 180~185

Stephan Schmitz
www.stephan-schmitz.ch
Page · 088~093

Sveta Dorosheva
www.behance.net/lattona
Page · 118~123

Taku Bannai
www.bannaitaku.jp
Page · 186~191

Teresa Bellon
teresabellon.tumblr.com
Page · 104~109

Tiago Galo
www.tiagogalo.com
Page · 164~169

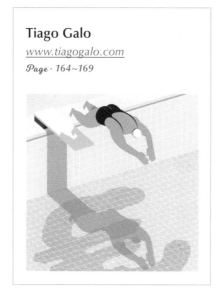

Tina Siuda
www.tinasiuda.com
Page · 230~232

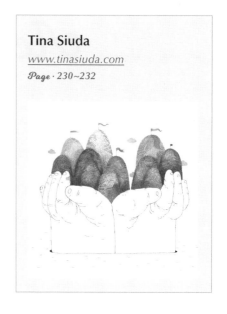

Tristan Gion
www.behance.net/tristan-gion
Page · 158~163

Whooli Chen
www.behance.net/whoolichen
Page · 010~017

Acknowledgements

We would like to thank all of the artists involved for granting us permission to publish their works. We are also very grateful to many other people whose names do not appear in the credits but who made specific contributions and provided support. Without these people, we would not have been able to share these beautiful works with readers around the world. Our editorial team includes editor Jessie Tan and book designer Dingding Huo, to whom we are truly grateful.